Lessons from the Sidelines

Karen R. Blake, MBA

ISBN 979-8-88616-743-6 (paperback)
ISBN 979-8-88616-744-3 (digital)

Christian Faith Publishing
832 Park Avenue
Meadville, PA 16335
www.christianfaithpublishing.com

Acknowledgments

First and foremost, I want to thank God and His only Son, Jesus Christ, for loving me enough to give me the time to finish what He started in me.

Next, thank you to my loving family, Stephen, James, and William, for who were the inspirations for this book and my own understanding.

Thank you to my friends, Carla Pierce and Anita Reason, for never letting me stray too far from achieving my goals by offering a caring word, a compassionate shoulder to lean on, or a quick kick in the pants when all else failed.

Lastly, to all of the amazing women who served as my inspiration to never give up on your dreams or your talent: my mom, Linda James Junior, Mia Rederick, Rita Baker-Schmidt, and the Women's Entrepreneurs of Baltimore.

Introduction

I have been blessed with the gift of a loving husband and two amazing sons. Now, if you had asked me twenty years ago what my life would be like, the reality of the first sentence of this paragraph would not have been on the list. By my late twenties, most of my closest friends were on their first marriages and starting their families. I was still discovering my career path and moving from one apartment to the next. Then came Stephen Keith Blake, and the rest, as they say, is history.

Shortly after we met and married, along came the first of two wonderful, healthy boys. Starting around age four, Stephen started what would become a quarterly habit of registering our children for one sport activity after another. It began innocently enough with T-Ball at the local YMCA; followed by swimming, baseball, lacrosse, a short attempt at football, basketball, soccer, wrestling, and ice hockey. With the passing of each season, I have watched a variety of sports equipment accumulate all over my house, become outgrown before the end of the season, my refrigerator covered with game and snack schedules and magnets with my children's smiling faces in their clean uniforms of whatever sport they were playing at the time.

The main reason that adults want their children to participate in organize sports is to teach some of the lessons of character that they will carry with them into adulthood. Lessons that are best learned through experience, like teamwork, self-sacrifice, working to achieve a goal, persistence, learning when to lead and when to follow, be prepared, and follow through. Recently, through my sleep deprived haze, I have begun to equate and translate some of this skills and lessons that the many volunteer coaches have shared with my children as to how they can be applied to everyday life.

Lesson 1

*Whenever possible, beat
your coach to practice.*

One is as dedicated to the preparation and execution of a team than the coach. Nothing speaks louder of one's dedication to the team more than being the first one to arrive to practice and the last one to leave. While the boys waited for the coach, they put on their cleats, took out their equipment, and started to warm up by jogging around the field.

Real-Time Application

A staff meeting has been called. You are the first one at the meeting table with your notebook open, pen out, and checking your calendar and emails on your smartphone. When the meeting ends, you are the last one to leave the room after re-checking your notes and chatting with the meeting organizer and fellow staff members.

James asked me, "Are you sure that I have practice today?" No one had yet arrived.

Lesson 2

*Assume there is practice unless
you have been told otherwise.*

Unless the boys received a phone call, text, email, or smoke signal from the coach or team mom; practice happened. Usually twice per week, regardless of traffic jams, snow, drizzling rain, and setting sun; practice happened. I think that the emphasis of practice was to teach that the game would happen in these conditions, so you might as well learn how to play in it. The greater purpose of practice was to teach to follow through in all circumstances (weather delays, late referees, the other team not showing up or not having enough players).

The other benefits of practice are the following:

1. Practice is where you learn new skills without jeopardizing the success of the team.
2. Practice is where individuals create shared experiences that begin to gel them into a team.
3. Practice is where/when you don't have the pressure of the real game, but how well you practice will affect the success of the team during the real game.
4. It is during practice that the coach can gauge a player's attitude and team cohesiveness.

Real-Time Application

You and your team have been given a project that has to be completed by a specific date for a presentation. Members of the team have contributed, but one has not due to a sudden illness. As the team coordinator, it is your responsibility to fill in the gaps (work late hours, find another team member, and redistribute the workload to the rest of the team or do the work yourself) but the project must be completed on time.

To the left, William playing with the Towson
Recreational Council, as Pitcher for the Volcanoes.
William played pitcher, short stop, and back catcher
for the same team during the same game.

Lesson 3

Little League is the perfect environment to try everything because everyone (until proven otherwise) can play every position.

During one particular baseball game, our youngest son, Will, played back catcher, short stop, and pitcher all in the same game for the same team. If you have the opportunity, volunteer for an organization that you care about and offer to do whatever the organization needs help with. Believe it or not, you may find hidden talents that you never knew you were capable of or with proper training, are able to develop.

There are so many fantastic nonprofit organizations that are starving for capable, competent, and consistent help, that the offer to "do whatever needs doing" is like music to their ears. If you decide to volunteer, try not to over commit. It is better to do a little consistently than to promise more than you can deliver. Also ask if you can be trained in an area that you are considering as a career path. Example, you are interested in social media, offer to set up and maintain a Facebook and Twitter page for the organization.

There are many advantages to volunteering:

1. Volunteering allows the staff to access your skills and make a determination on the best placement and use of those skills
2. It allows the volunteers to try something new without feeling locked in to any one position.
3. When a volunteer does well, it gives him/her confidence. If the placement is successful, the volunteer knows that they can move on to something else without the burden of the success of the organization on their shoulders.

Real-Time Application

Recently, I had a volunteer who offered to do whatever the organization needed, but she didn't have many skills (according to her). I asked her if she had ever worked on a computer, she said *yes*. Great. Let's try data entry. Three weeks later, the volunteer had entered all of my volunteer records into Microsoft Access, and she had new skills to add to her resume. Win-win.

Lesson 4

*There are times when it is best
to make the first move.*

Our youngest son, Will, was wrestling in an end of
the season tournament. His opponent had gotten the
first take down (two points). They went into double
overtime. His opponent won the match on a techni-
cality because he had earned the first takedown.

The problem in making the first move in life
and in business is that you are never sure if you are
exposing yourself to unforeseen forces that could
take advantage of you. The risk could bring about
rewards later.

Real-Time Application

You can feel more confident about when to make the first move in life and business if you have a trusted coach or mentor to guide you. It is best to confer with your coach or mentor who is more familiar with the rules and strategies of the game before your turn on the mat.

Lesson 5

*Whenever possible, own
your own equipment.*

The decision to invest in the purchasing of equipment for children who have no idea if they are going to stick with a particular activity is unnerving. Basically, most types of teams-recreational, travel, high school, and middle school, will supply the main equipment (bats, balls, back catcher pads, and helmets). But the other equipment-sport appropriate footwear, lacrosse sticks, mouth guards, and uniforms are up to the participants.

The investment of one's own equipment really is an investment in personal development. When you have your equipment, you can practice on your own which can help enhance your skills come game time.

Real-Time Application

Whenever possible, own your own books and magazine subscriptions that support your professional and personal development. Own whatever you need to walk into any situation prepared to compete.

Lesson 6

Learn your sport from those who have proven that they better than you.

Summer camps, watching professionals, and watching those who are performing at the next level from you (JV, varsity, professional) all play a part in the learning curve of any skill. Whenever possible, wherever possible, watch c-span, financial advice programs, city cable, and go to the library and take out books (free) on subjects that interest you.

The greatest learning technique for anything is doing. Do the job under the watchful eye of a compassionate mentor that you trust to tell you the truth.

Example

James and William have increased their knowledge and physical ability with every opportunity to play any given sport during that sports off-season. Both have attended summer soccer, lacrosse, and tennis camps. Let us not forget summer academic enrichment courses such as math and English (the jury is still out on the benefits of those classes).

Real-Time Application

Whenever possible, time and financially, go to as many workshops and seminars that you can to improve yourself personally and professionally. With each new exposure, you gain new ideas, new ways of looking at problems or circumstances, and learn new ways to solve problems.

Also when you work with someone who knows more than you, you can ask the questions that they may have already gained the answer through personal experience. That my friend is called wisdom, thereby cutting length of your learning curve.

Lesson 7

Always do your best with no expectations. Do your best and when magic happens, buy the T-shirt.

In life, there are no guarantees. However, some understood situations and life values seem to bring about positive results, such as not becoming involved with illegal narcotics and overindulgence of almost anything (food, alcohol, and shopping). Doing ones, best in school, telling the truth, and being loyal towards one's friends and family, are all personal decisions that serve as a guidepost for one's life.

A question will arise when "bad things happen to good people," why did a bad situation happen? If you are a good person, who is trying to do your personal best, are not good things supposed to happen? As I mentioned in the previous paragraph, in life, there are no guarantees, just opportunities to better know oneself. Are you good because good things happen for you or are you good because you have done your best?

Example

It was the spring of 2005 lacrosse season when the Maryland Lacrosse Club, Boys Lightening B team participated in the end of the season tournament known as LAXSPLASH. The seasons' record going into the tournament was six wins, three losses, and one tie. There were twenty-eight teams entered in the B division, three of which were all-star teams specifically recruited for this tournament.

At the time of the tournament, of the sixteen boys on the team, at least seven of them had played together on various teams for at least two years. No one on this team had ever made it to the finals of LAXSPLASH, so the possibility that we could actually make it past the first round was, well, remote. Our coach, Doug DeSchmit, sent an email detailing the weekend tournament schedule. At the end of the email, he noted that "there is always potential of playing Sunday morning if we win two games;" in other words, be prepared to play two games, and do not get your hopes up for anything more. Okay.

MLC went on to win all five games over the course of two days. The championship game was played against an all-star team. MLC went on to win the championship the final score was 10-8. Winning the championship was really just an external manifestation of an internal relationship. Many of the young men on the team were classmates, friends, and teammates for other sports. During the course of the tournament, every person on the team (except the goalie) scored, even the defensemen! It was a completely pure and selfless experience.

After the final game, my husband went straight to the tent where tournament paraphilia was being sold; he bought a tournament T-shirt. My first reaction was to say, "James is going to receive a championship T-shirt, you do not need to buy one." Upon reflection, I am glad that he bought the T-shirt. To date, each child's lacrosse team continues to enter the end of the year tournament but have not yet made it back to the finals. Every time I see the T-shirt, usually in the laundry after being worn as a nightshirt, I am reminded of an unexpected happy moment when ordinary kids came together and did something special.

Real-Time Application

Never assume that the other person or team is better than you are. Never assume an outcome. If you have been asked or volunteered to accomplish a task, prepare yourself to perform at your best, then execute.

Everyone on the team can contribute something to achieving the goal. *Everyone.* When the task has been completed, take a moment to reflect and appreciate the effort no matter the outcome.

Lesson 8

When someone is injured on the field, everybody stop and take a knee.

Keep the activities of life in perspective (work, play, and achievements). The business world is completive, but you never genuinely want someone to be seriously injured. Everyone is working to achieve the best outcome for them but not at the cost of permanently eliminating their competition. Keep winning in perspective.

When a competitor is injured, take a moment to hope for their recovery, clap when they get back on their feet, and get back into the game. You will be better for the genuine competition.

Example

Whenever a child is injured, everyone stops, bends down on one knee, and waits for the injured person to get back on their feet.

Real-Time Application

People experience difficulties all of the time. Sometimes life can knock you on your backside. If you know that someone is having a hard time, and you can genuinely help them in some tangible way, do it. At some point in your life, you may need someone to help you up.

Lesson 9

*If you sign up to bring a
snack, follow through.*

I cannot begin to express the disappointment the
players feel when something has been scheduled but
does not occur. If you volunteer for something, do all
that you can to follow through. If you are not able to
follow through (flat tire, the kids get sick in the car,
and you are called into work), have a plan B; have a
team roster with the parents' cell phone numbers to
ask someone to switch with you.

Know that most kids will eat grapes, pretzels,
and juice boxes. Though you cannot please everyone, try to; you don't want to unnecessarily exclude
anyone. There have been quite a few incidents that I
have, after realizing that the parent who was scheduled to bring the snack was not at the game, made

a mad dash to the nearest grocery store to buy thirty-two bags of assorted chips and two cases of juice boxes before the end of the second half.

Volunteering has the ability to share your gifts and talents with those who have no expectations of you until you do it. What volunteering exposes is a person's true character; are they a person of their word, and if things don't go as planned, will they do everything they can to solve the problem?

Real-Time Application

As a professional who has worked with volunteers for over twenty years, I have seen people do wonderful things because it was in their heart to do so: volunteer coaches and soup kitchen volunteers who feed and clothe the needy. But I have also seen those who "volunteered" only because they were forced: court ordered or for credit for an academic class. However, a person came to volunteer is really not the point, rather, what did they show and share with those around them while they volunteered.

Were they warm, welcoming, and willing to do whatever was needed? Or were they argumentative, difficult to get along with, and always hiding from work? Volunteering can be an opportunity to discover gifts and talents that may otherwise not had a chance to be explored.

If you are considering a career change or want to express your personal beliefs in a tangible way, consider volunteering with a local nonprofit.

Lesson 10

*No matter what, be your
kid's biggest fan.*

No matter how amazing your child may be, they will not always win. Good. Learning how to be a gracious loser is just as important as being a humble winner. At all times, as a child's adult example, show them that they are appreciated for their efforts, and not necessarily the results. It is from those genuine spontaneous moments of unconditional support that lend to the encouragement of the continued pursuit of excellence.

Real-Time Application

At work or through the day, share the positives of life. Regardless of the office environment, genuine positive feedback is always appropriate and mostly needed. It would be wonderful if human beings could mentally leave home at home and work and work; unfortunately, life, for most of us, does not work that way. One never knows when a word of genuine praise or encouragement will be just what a person needs to make it through the day on a positive note.

Closing

In closing, these top ten life lessons have been presented, refined, and lived over the course of the past twenty years of marriage and parenthood. That's not to say that I did not know these truths before this phase of my life, but I don't think I was fully aware of them as when I had to teach them to our children.

Let's have a recap:

- Whenever possible, beat your coach to practice
- Assume there is a practice unless you have been told otherwise
- Little league is the perfect environment to try everything because everyone (until proven otherwise) can play every position
- There are times when it is best to make the first move
- Own your own equipment

- Learn your sport from those who have proven than they are better than you
- Always do your best with no exceptions. Do your best and when magic happens, buy the T-shirt
- When someone is injured on the field, everybody stop and take a knee
- If you sign up to bring a snack, follow through
- No matter what, be your kid's biggest fan.

What does it all mean? Well, it depends on the circumstance that you are in at any given time. A real time application could be is that when a volunteer asked me to speak in front of his congregation on behalf a nonprofit organization, I agreed to do so. If I could not follow through, then I better be responsible enough to let the organizer know so that other arrangements could be made (Lesson 9).

As a volunteer coordinator, it is my job to recruit, train, place, motivate, and retain the best volunteers and place them in the right position where their gifts and talents will be used for the benefit of the organization and the volunteer will feel successful. Sometimes, that goal takes a few experiments until the right fit is achieved. But that is the opportunity that volunteering brings; experimentation until you find the right fit. Recently, I had a volunteer who had never done data entry. I asked if she had ever used a computer; her answer was *yes*. So, we tried it out; she did fine (Lesson 3).

It is my hope that these lessons will benefit you by bringing more:

- Cooperation
- Preparation
- Dedication
- Determination
- Introspection
- Opportunities
- Skills
- Character
- Vision for your life and a path to achieve that life
- Perspective
- Community
- Peace

I do not know what other life lessons my family will reveal to me, only that I am open to the learning and application of whatever tomorrow may bring.

Notes

KAREN R. BLAKE, MBA

About the Author

 Karen R. Blake, MBA is a native Baltimorean. She lives with her husband and child in Baltimore. She also owns and operates a non-profit consulting firm, Certified Non-Profit Consulting, LLC which is specializing in volunteer management. She is a past president of the Rotary Club of Baltimore. She serves on various non-profit boards. She is a brain cancer survivor. In addition, she holds a master's in business administration from University of Maryland University College.

www.ingramcontent.com/pod-product-compliance
Lightning Source LLC
Chambersburg PA
CBHW040204160726
48006CB00014B/1892